PRAISE FOR THE BROADWAY PRODUCTION OF
HEDWIG AND THE ANGRY INCH

"Harris is beyond fabulous, holds nothing back and plays it anyway but safe in Michael Mayer's exhilarating production . . . The beauty of Mitchell and Trask's show is that it takes the strangest of bedfellows—camp, punk and pathos—and blends them into something unexpectedly poignant."

—DAVID ROONEY, *The Hollywood Reporter*

"Neil Patrick Harris simply crushes it . . . the songs 'Wicked Little Town,' 'Origin of Love' and 'Wig in a Box' deserve to be on iPods everywhere." —MARK KENNEDY, *Associated Press*

"Mr. Harris is in full command of who he is and, most excitingly, what he has become with this performance. That's a bona fide Broadway star, the kind who can rule an audience with the blink of a sequined eyelid . . . *Hedwig* is a shamelessly enjoyable show." —BEN BRANTLEY, *The New York Times*

"For all the cleverness of the book and the pathos of Hedwig the character, this is a true rock concert . . . Harris's bravura performance manages to integrate about 30 years of rock musical styles . . . a spectacular revival."

—MARILYN STASIO, *Variety*

"[In] John Cameron Mitchell and Stephen Trask's brilliant rock musical . . . Harris offers up a bravura, frequently thrilling, deeply committed, self-pushing performance . . ."

—CHRIS JONES, *Chicago Tribune*

HEDWIG
and the
ANGRY INCH

HEDWIG
ANGRY INCH

Book by
John Cameron Mitchell

Music & Lyrics by
Stephen Trask

OVERLOOK DUCKWORTH
NEW YORK • LONDON

This edition first published in the United States and the United Kingdom in 2014 by
Overlook Duckworth, Peter Mayer Publishers, Inc., New York

NEW YORK:
141 Wooster Street
New York, NY 10012
www.overlookpress.com
For bulk and special sales, please contact sales@overlookpress.com,
or write to us at the address above.

LONDON:
30 Calvin Street
London E1 6NW
info@duckworth-publishers.co.uk
www.duckworth.co.uk
For bulk and special sales, please contact sales@duckworth-publishers.co.uk,
or write to us at the address above.

Cataloging-in-Publication Data is available from the Library of Congress

BOOK DESIGN AND FORMATTING BY BERNARD SCHLEIFER
Manufactured in the United States of America
ISBN 978-1-4683-1002-3 (US)
ISBN 978-0-7156-4938-1 (UK)
5 7 9 10 8 6 4

AUTHORS' NOTE

This script is, at best, a record of a single evening of a single production of *Hedwig and the Angry Inch.* We deliberately developed it over a number of years in non-theatrical venues—rock clubs, drag bars, birthday parties, friends' patios—in order to keep it free-flowing, improvisational, alive. We encourage other productions to keep this sense of freedom by ad-libbing when appropriate within the confines of the world of the piece. This script reflects that we were performing on Broadway at the Belasco Theatre. Tommy was therefore appearing in nearby Times Square. (The play may be set in the present or past at director's discretion.) We feel that every production should be site-specific so that the character of Hedwig is actually performing in and commenting on the space the production is occupying. Feel free to change the text to accommodate the environment. The authors simply require that the changes be hilarious.

JOHN CAMERON MITCHELL
STEPHEN TRASK

HEDWIG
and the
ANGRY INCH

Hedwig and the Angry Inch premiered on Broadway at the Belasco Theatre in New York City on April 22, 2014. Book by John Cameron Mitchell; Music and Lyrics by Stephen Trask.

The cast was as follows:

HEDWIG	Neil Patrick Harris
YITZHAK	Lena Hall

THE ANGRY INCH:

SKSZP (Guitar, Keyboards, Vocals)	Justin Craig
JACEK (Bass, Guitar, Keyboards, Vocals)	Matt Duncan
KRZYZHTOFF (Guitar, Vocals)	Tim Mislock
SCHLATKO (Drums, Vocals)	Peter Yanowitz

Director: Michael Mayer
Musical Staging: Spencer Liff
Scenic Design: Julian Crouch
Costume Design: Arianne Phillips
Lighting Design: Kevin Adams
Wig and Make-up Design: Mike Potter
Sound Design: Tim O'Heir
Projection Design: Benjamin Pearcy for 59 Productions
Animation Design: John Bair
Casting: Calleri Casting
Music Supervisor and Coordinator: Ethan Popp
Music Director: Justin Craig
Vocal Supervisor: Liz Caplan

This production was produced on Broadway by David Binder, Jayne Baron Sherman, Barbara Whitman, Latitude Link, Patrick Catullo, Raise the Roof, Paula Marie Black, Colin Callender, Ruth Hendel, Sharon Karmazin, Martian Entertainment, Stacey Mindich, Eric Schnall, and The Shubert Organization

Executive Producer: 101 Productions, Ltd.
Associate Producer: Mark Berger

Hedwig and the Angry Inch was originally presented at the Westbeth Theatre Center on February 27, 1997, by David Binder. It was presented off-Broadway at the Jane Street Theatre on February 14, 1998, by Peter Askin, Susann Brinkley, James B. Freydberg. Directed by Peter Askin; Set Design by James Youmans; Lighting Design by Kevin Adams.

The cast was as follows:

HEDWIG	John Cameron Mitchell
THE ANGRY INCH	Cheater
Comprised of Stephen Trask, Chris Weilding, Dave McKinley, Scott Bilbrey	
YITZHAK	Miriam Shor

(A Broadway theater. Onstage is a set depicting a modern Middle Eastern street in ruins. A huge bomb crater takes up most of stage. In the center is a blown-out wreck of a car with bits of exploding vehicle hanging in mid-air as a tableau vivant. Warming up onstage is The Angry Inch, a rock band dressed flashily but affordably. YITZHAK, *a sullen male roadie, trudges to the center-stage mic. He speaks with a Croatian accent.)*

YITZHAK

Welcome to the Belasco Theatre. Before the show starts, please turn off all cellular telephones and surveillance devices. It's a loud show, but there are some quiet bits and, trust me, you don't want to be that person with this bitch.

Ladies and gentleman, whether you like it or not . . . Hedwig!

("America the Beautiful" begins on Hendrixy guitar and HEDWIG *enters by parachute.)*

HEDWIG

DON'T YOU KNOW ME?
I'M THE NEW BERLIN WALL.
TRY AND TEAR ME DOWN!

TEAR ME DOWN

HEDWIG

I WAS BORN ON THE OTHER SIDE
OF A TOWN RIPPED IN TWO
I MADE IT OVER THE GREAT DIVIDE
NOW I'M COMING FOR YOU

ENEMIES AND ADVERSARIES
THEY TRY AND TEAR ME DOWN
YOU WANT ME, BABY, I DARE YOU
TRY AND TEAR ME DOWN

I ROSE FROM OFF OF THE DOCTOR'S SLAB
LIKE LAZARUS FROM THE PIT
NOW EVERYONE WANTS TO TAKE A STAB
AND DECORATE ME
WITH BLOOD GRAFFITI AND SPIT

ENEMIES AND ADVERSARIES
THEY TRY AND TEAR ME DOWN
YOU WANT ME, BABY, I DARE YOU
TRY AND TEAR ME DOWN

YITZHAK

ON AUGUST 13, 1961,
A WALL WAS ERECTED
DOWN THE MIDDLE OF THE CITY OF BERLIN.
THE WORLD WAS DIVIDED BY A COLD WAR
AND THE BERLIN WALL
WAS THE MOST HATED SYMBOL OF THAT DIVIDE
REVILED. GRAFFITIED. SPIT UPON.
WE THOUGHT THE WALL WOULD STAND FOREVER.
AND NOW THAT IT'S GONE
WE DON'T KNOW WHO WE ARE ANYMORE.
LADIES AND GENTLEMAN,
HEDWIG IS LIKE THAT WALL,
STANDING BEFORE YOU IN THE DIVIDE
BETWEEN EAST AND WEST,
SLAVERY AND FREEDOM,
MAN AND WOMAN,
TOP AND BOTTOM.
AND YOU CAN TRY AND TEAR HER DOWN,
BUT BEFORE YOU DO,
YOU MUST REMEMBER ONE THING

HEDWIG

LISTEN

THERE AIN'T MUCH OF A DIFFERENCE

BETWEEN A BRIDGE AND A WALL

WITHOUT ME RIGHT IN THE MIDDLE, BABE

YOU WOULD BE NOTHING AT ALL

ENEMIES AND ADVERSARIES

THEY TRY AND TEAR ME DOWN

YOU WANT ME, BABY, I DARE YOU

TRY AND TEAR ME DOWN

ENEMIES AND ADVERSARIES

THEY TRY AND TEAR ME DOWN

YOU WANT ME, BABY, I DARE YOU

TRY AND TEAR ME DOWN

FROM EAST BERLIN

TO JUNCTION CITY

HELLO NEW YORK!

HELLO NEW JERSEY!

WHAT? YOU WANNA TRY AND TEAR ME DOWN?

COME ON AND TEAR ME . . .

YITZHAK

(Echoing and outdoing HEDWIG *vocally.)*

COME ON AND TEAR ME . . .

(HEDWIG pulls the cable out of YITZHAK's mic.)

HEDWIG

COME ON AND TEAR ME DOWN!

(Arena rock finish.)

Thank you! Thank you, you're so sweet. I do love a warm hand on my entrance. My name is Hedwig.

(Referring to the band.)

Please welcome The Angry Inch! And my husband and Man Friday through Thursday, Yitzhak!

(On the applause . . .)

There's no need . . . *(Silencing the audience.)* There's none!

I'm thrilled you could join me for this special one-night-only performance here at the beautiful Belasco Theatre. Look at me. On Broadway! Well, Broadway Adjacent. East of Broadway. E-Bra. Welcome to E-Bra, ladies and gentlemen.

We are here tonight courtesy of Bob Wankel of the Shubert Organization. On bended knee did I beg Bob for my Broadway debut. He told me not to talk with my mouth full.

(She falls suddenly to the floor boards and begins to stroke them.)

I'm moved, ladies and gentlemen. I'm moved by the simple fact that this . . . *(Refers to her body.)* . . . cruelly abridged corpus is at this very moment being supported by the same groaning planks that cradled Brando's debut and Barrymore's farewell. Where Tim Curry cracked wise and Mark Rylance batted his eyes . . .

(She licks the floor.)

Tastes like Kathy Griffin. Wow.

(She stands and touches the proscenium.)

History lesson. David Belasco built this theater in 1907. The Bishop of Broadway they called him, as he was always dressed in priestly attire. They say if his ghost appears at your opening night you'll be a hit. His customary seat was in that box.

(Points to a certain box and addresses an audience member seated there.)

Sir, will you keep a look out? If you're touched by a priest, for God sake, speak up.

(Back to the audience.)

Imagine me in the birthplace of *Awake and Sing*, *A Raisin in the Sun*, and most recently . . . *Hurt Locker: The Musical*, which opened last night and closed at intermission. Bob Wankel persuaded them to let us have the set for one more night before they strike it. Once again . . . *(mouth full)* . . . thanks, Bob. Think of me as a theatrical hermit crab. Welcome to my new shell. How's it look on me?

(On applause.)

You legitimize me, ladies and gentlemen. You really do. But let's be honest. Many of you here have only recently become aware of me . . .

(She refers to a projection: a NY Post *newspaper cover dominated by a police mugshot of a bandaged young man with the remnant of a silver cross smeared on his forehead. The man bears a remarkable likeness to* HEDWIG. *The headline reads: "TOMMY TO TOTS: SORRY!")*

It took a tragedy to make you finally pay attention. But now you're interested. Intrigued, even.

(Projection zooms to a tiny box at the bottom of the page featuring a smiling mugshot of a bandaged HEDWIG *with the caption, "Who is Mystery Woman?" Then, in a broad American accent:)*

"Who is this Hedwig and why have we never heard about her before, Jerry?"

(Normal accent.)

Well, that's a question I've been asking myself for years. How did some slip of a girlyboy from communist East Berlin become the internationally ignored song stylist barely standing before you? That's what I want to talk about tonight. I'm not here to talk about calamity or scandal. I'm not here to talk about my relationship with a certain well-known rock icon, Tommy Gnosis . . .

(Projection: zoom to TOMMY *'s mugshot.* HEDWIG *walks upstage, pushes aside some scenery pieces and pulls down a drop to reveal an emergency exit door on the bare brick back wall of the theater.)*

HEDWIG

. . . even though, at this very moment, he's probably talking about me. By some freak coincidence, he's launching his "Tour of Atonement" tonight in Times Square . . .

*(*HEDWIG *kicks open the door. We hear thousands cheering . . .)*

TOMMY *(Off.)*

Hello New York! Listen . . . listen . . . there's someone else I want to thank for the way they've handled this tragedy . . . with incredible loyalty in the face of a lot of lies. And that someone is . . .

*(*HEDWIG *is excited about her imminent shout-out . . .)*

. . . you! My fans!

(Cheers. Her face falls. A synthesized intro to "Tear Me Down" begins.)

And together, no one's gonna tear us down!

(Sings.)

ENEMIES AND ADVERSARIES

*(*HEDWIG *slams the door.)*

HEDWIG

I wrote every song on that album! And BTW, TMZ got it right. He *was* driving, he *was* on blow, he *was* getting blown by yours truly, and he *did* hit the schoolbus full of deaf children, one survived—now blind. I taught him everything he knows and has apparently forgotten about rock and roll and he barely mentions my name on that giant sucking sound Anderson Cooper calls a show, which I'm sure you all saw because if you hadn't, I'd be singing to the Bishop and, if I was lucky, my manager Phyllis Stein—did you make it this time, Phyllis?

(She's overcome.)

I'm sorry. I'm wide open tonight. You're lookin' at a locker full of hurt.

You see, ladies and gentleman, the road is my home. My home, the road. And when I think of all the people I have come upon in my travels, I have to think about the people who have come upon me.

The geography of human contact, the triangulation of a pair of eyes on my face, the latitude and longitude of a hand on my body. These are the only clues I have to my place in the world. To who I am. Who is Mystery Woman!? *(Laughs.)* I laugh, because I will cry if I don't.

I recently found my first diary, age 2 through 6—fully illustrated —and I realized that so many people have touched me on my way to this stage tonight. How can I say who touched me the most? My father? . . . The American GI who left when I was barely old enough to speak my first words: "Daddy, when I grow up, I'll kill you"? Could it have been my East German mother? No, when she touched me it was usually by accident. One day, we were watching *Jesus Christ Superstar* on American Forces Television. I turned to Mother:

(As CHILD:) "Jesus said the darndest things."

She slapped me.

(As MOM:) "Don't you ever mention that name to me again!"

(As CHILD:) "But He died for our sins."

(As MOM:) "So did Hitler."

(As CHILD:) "What?"

(As MOM:) "Absolute power corrupts."

(As CHILD:) "Absolutely!"

(As MOM:) "Better to be powerless, my son."

When the Wall went up, her wish came true. We happened to be living on the East side and Mother was given a job teaching sculpture to limbless children. Socialism, God rest its soul . . .

Most of my time was spent listening to American Forces Radio. Our apartment was so small that Mother made me play it in the oven. Late at night, I would rest my head on the top rack . . .

(She rests her head under the car hood and reverb is added to her voice as if she were in an oven.)

. . . and listen to the American Masters . . . Toni Tennille . . . Debby Boone . . . Anne Murray—who was actually a Canadian working in the American idiom. Then there were the crypto-homo rockers: Lou Reed . . . Iggy Pop . . . David Bowie—who was actually an idiom working in America and Canada. These artists left as deep an impression on me as that oven rack did on my face. To be a young American in muskrat love, soft as an easy chair, not even the chair—I am, I said! Have I never been mellow?

(Singing.)

HAVE I NEVER TRIED?

And the colored girls sing . . .

*(*YITZHAK *sings backup vocals from Lou Reed's "Walk on the Wild Side.")*

YITZHAK

DOO DO DOO . . .

HEDWIG

I sang along . . .

YITZHAK AND HEDWIG

. . . DOO DO DOO . . .

HEDWIG

But never with the melody. How could I do it better than Toni or Lou?

YITZHAK

. . . DOO DO DOO . . .

HEDWIG

Once I couldn't resist singing the lead . . .

(Singing from Debby Boone's "You Light Up My Life.")

IT CAN'T BE WRONG, WHEN IT FEELS SO RIGH—!"

Mother threw a tomato at my head.

YITZHAK

. . . DOO DO DOO . . .

HEDWIG

But I was quite content to sing gentle backup harmonies in my oven.

YITZHAK

. . . DOO DO DOO . . .

HEDWIG

. . . while Mother sculpted in the shower.

YITZHAK

DOO DO DOO . . .

(YITZHAK stops singing.)

HEDWIG

When the hour grew late and it was time for bed, she would shout from the bathroom, "Well, that's me!" And I would reply from the kitchen, "Well, I guess that's me too." We would wash our feet and brush our teeth and lay down on the narrow pallet that we had shared since Daddy left . . . like two pieces of a puzzle that don't quite fit but are jammed together and left on a table by . . .

(Railing at the heavens.)

. . . some dangerous shut-in with too much time on his hands!

(Overcome again.)

I'm sorry, I'm completely dilated right now.

(The gentle guitar intro of "The Origin of Love" begins.)

I'd like to share with you a bedtime story that Mother once whispered to me in the dark, and later retracted. Whatever allowed her to reveal such a story to such a little boy, I'll never know. But I remember it like it happened yesterday.

THE ORIGIN OF LOVE

(Animation projected on a downstage scrim illustrates the story.)

WHEN THE EARTH WAS STILL FLAT,
AND CLOUDS MADE OF FIRE,
AND MOUNTAINS STRETCHED UP TO THE SKY,
SOMETIMES HIGHER,
FOLKS ROAMED THE EARTH
LIKE BIG ROLLING KEGS.
THEY HAD TWO SETS OF ARMS.
THEY HAD TWO SETS OF LEGS.
THEY HAD TWO FACES PEERING
OUT OF ONE GIANT HEAD
SO THEY COULD WATCH ALL AROUND THEM
AS THEY TALKED; WHILE THEY READ.
AND THEY NEVER KNEW NOTHING OF LOVE.
IT WAS BEFORE THE ORIGIN OF LOVE.

THE ORIGIN OF LOVE

AND THERE WERE THREE SEXES THEN,
ONE THAT LOOKED LIKE TWO MEN
GLUED UP BACK TO BACK,
CALLED THE CHILDREN OF THE SUN.
AND SIMILAR IN SHAPE AND GIRTH
WERE THE CHILDREN OF THE EARTH

THEY LOOKED LIKE TWO GIRLS
ROLLED UP IN ONE.
AND THE CHILDREN OF THE MOON
WERE LIKE A FORK SHOVED ON A SPOON.
THEY WERE PART SUN, PART EARTH,
PART DAUGHTER, PART SON.

THE ORIGIN OF LOVE.

NOW THE GODS GREW QUITE SCARED
OF OUR STRENGTH AND DEFIANCE
AND THOR SAID,
"I'M GONNA KILL THEM ALL
WITH MY HAMMER,
LIKE I KILLED THE GIANTS."
AND ZEUS SAID, "NO,
YOU BETTER LET ME
USE MY LIGHTNING, LIKE SCISSORS,
LIKE I CUT THE LEGS OFF THE WHALES
AND DINOSAURS INTO LIZARDS."
THEN HE GRABBED UP SOME BOLTS
AND HE LET OUT A LAUGH,
SAID, "I'LL SPLIT THEM RIGHT DOWN THE MIDDLE.
GONNA CUT THEM RIGHT UP IN HALF."
AND THEN STORM CLOUDS GATHERED ABOVE
INTO GREAT BALLS OF FIRE

AND THEN FIRE SHOT DOWN
FROM THE SKY IN BOLTS
LIKE SHINING BLADES
OF A KNIFE.
AND IT RIPPED
RIGHT THROUGH THE FLESH
OF THE CHILDREN OF THE SUN
AND THE MOON
AND THE EARTH.
AND SOME INDIAN GOD
SEWED THE WOUND UP INTO A HOLE,
PULLED IT ROUND TO OUR BELLY
TO REMIND US OF THE PRICE WE PAY.
AND OSIRIS AND THE GODS OF THE NILE
GATHERED UP A BIG STORM
TO BLOW A HURRICANE,
TO SCATTER US AWAY,
IN A FLOOD OF WIND AND RAIN,
AND A SEA OF TIDAL WAVES,
TO WASH US ALL AWAY,
AND IF WE DON'T BEHAVE
THEY'LL CUT US DOWN AGAIN
AND WE'LL BE HOPPING AROUND ON ONE FOOT
AND LOOKING THROUGH ONE EYE.

LAST TIME I SAW YOU
WE HAD JUST SPLIT IN TWO.

YOU WERE LOOKING AT ME.

I WAS LOOKING AT YOU.

YOU HAD A WAY SO FAMILIAR,

BUT I COULD NOT RECOGNIZE,

'CAUSE YOU HAD BLOOD ON YOUR FACE;

I HAD BLOOD IN MY EYES.

BUT I COULD SWEAR BY YOUR EXPRESSION

THAT THE PAIN DOWN IN YOUR SOUL

WAS THE SAME AS THE ONE DOWN IN MINE.

THAT'S THE PAIN,

CUTS A STRAIGHT LINE

DOWN THROUGH THE HEART;

WE CALLED IT LOVE.

SO WE WRAPPED OUR ARMS AROUND EACH OTHER

TRYING TO SHOVE OURSELVES BACK TOGETHER.

WE WERE MAKING LOVE,

MAKING LOVE.

IT WAS A COLD, DARK EVENING

SUCH A LONG TIME AGO,

WHEN BY THE MIGHTY HAND OF JOVE,

IT WAS A SAD STORY

HOW WE BECAME

LONELY TWO-LEGGED CREATURES

IT'S THE STORY OF

THE ORIGIN OF LOVE.

THAT'S THE ORIGIN OF LOVE.

(The song ends with the projection of an image of a broken eye. The scrim rises.)

Thank you. I do love a good scrim job.

After Mother finished her story, she began to snore. But I had to go somewhere I could think. I crept into the kitchen and put my head in the oven.

(Back under the car hood. Reverb.)

It is clear that I must find my other half. But is it a he or a she? Is it Daddy? He went away. Or Mother? I was suddenly afraid to go back to bed. What does this person look like? Identical to me? Or somehow complementary? Does my other half have what I don't? Did he get the looks? The luck? The love? Were we really separated forcibly or did he just run off with the good stuff? Or did I? Will this person embarrass me? And what about sex? Is that how we put ourselves back together again? Is that what Daddy was trying to—? Or can two people actually become one again? And if we're driving on the Autobahn when it happens, can we still use the diamond lane?

Practical questions. Of wholeness. Completion. Think of it. I thought of it. I thought of the power. The gods would be terrified!

(She sees YITZHAK *furtively stroking a wig. Furious . . .)*

Yitzhak! Was machst du da verdammt noch mal?

(YITZHAK *replaces the wig quickly.* HEDWIG *points into the house.)*

HEDWIG

Look, Yitzhak . . .

(YITZHAK *looks.)*

Immigration!

(YITZHAK *is alarmed then deflated as he realizes the "joke.")*

If you behave, I might let you shave my back. That will be all.

(HEDWIG *walks away.)*

I'm sorry you had to see that, ladies and gentlemen. When I met him he said he wanted to be a model. A foot model, maybe. How's my hair? It smells heavenly. It smells like the hands of seventy-five Bangladeshi children. Too soon? Too late.

(Up to no good, YITZHAK *opens the emergency door. The Tommy Gnosis concert pours in again.)*

TOMMY *(Off.)*

—I realized there was only one person who had ever really been there for me in my life . . .

*(*HEDWIG *is expectant.)*

And that person was me. The accident was a cry for help. I was yelling "Help!" to me.

(Outraged, HEDWIG *slams the door closed.)*

HEDWIG

WELL, WHAT ABOUT ME? Without me he never would've swerved into that oncoming shortbus and revived his moribund career with a well-timed redemption tale! Gag order be damned . . .

(She tells the story.)

It all went down in the newly annoying Meat-Packing District. MePa. I had just been barred from entering the Jane Hotel— apparently I'd left my Douche ID at home—when a limo pulled up. I hopped in, naturally mistaking it for my own.

(The band laughs derisively. She glares at them.)

Say it to my face. Say it to my face.

I will cut a bitch.

In the limo sat Tommy Gnosis. We were both astonished. It had been years. So we dropped the driver off and drove up and down the island, doing drugs and catching up. We talked about the disappointing sales of his sophomore album—the one he wrote without me. He spoke of his loneliness. I reminded him of happier days. I just couldn't keep my mouth shut and well, you know the rest. So you can imagine, when the story broke, Tommy's people offered me a small fortune to keep all this to myself. As if I'd accept their filthy lucre. As if selling a story of someone else's pain was my only means of support. As if I hadn't already launched my new fragrance: "Atrocity By Hedwig."

(Projection of "Atrocity" logo.)

It's a fragrance for a man or a woman. Or a man-woman. Or a woman-man. Or a moman. Or a wan.

I digress.

One day in the late mid eighties, I was in my early late twenties. I had just been dismissed from university after delivering a brilliant lecture on the aggressive influence of

German philosophy on rock and roll entitled: "You, Kant, Always Get What You Want. But If You Try Sometime, You Just Might Find, You Get What You Nietzsche."

At 26, my academic career was over, I had never kissed a boy and I was still sleeping with Mom. The search for my other half on this side of the Wall had proved futile. Might he be found on the other? But how to get over? People died trying. Such were the thoughts flooding my tiny head on the day that I was . . .

. . . sunning myself in an old bomb crater I had discovered near the Wall. I am naked, face down, on a piece of broken church, inhaling a fragrant westerly breeze. The new McDonald's has just opened on the other side. Good God, I deserve a break today. All I ever seem to get is the unhappy meal. And I'm not lovin' it.

The sun is hot, but I feel a sudden chill. I look over my shoulder. A head-shaped shadow is resting on the pillow of my ass.

> (AS LUTHER:) "Girl, I sure don't mean to annoy you, my name is Sargeant Luther Robinson."

I turn my body to face him.

> (AS HANSEL:) "My name is Hansel."

Luther is silent for a moment as he stares at my little bishop in a turtleneck.

(AS LUTHER:) "Hansel. Well, you must like candy."

(AS HANSEL:) "I like Gummi Baerchen."

Out of his pocket comes a strange, American-looking packet that says "Gummy Bears" on it. Gummy Bears? I select a single clear bear. It is the biggest one I've ever seen. The taste is completely different from a Gummi Bear, yet somehow familiar. It is much sweeter than a Gummi Bear and softer, too. Its little gummy body stretches on the rack of my molars. Wow, I feel so optimistic. He pours me a handful, his eyes heavy with an unfamiliar desire. Could it be a desire to please? Me? I suddenly recognize the flavor in my mouth. It's the taste of power. Not bad.

(AS LUTHER:) "Damn, Hansel, I can't believe you're not a girl, you're so fine. Why don't you take the whole bag?"

He searches my face for news of his fate. His expression is echoed in scores of tiny faces pressing against clear plastic. Panting faces of every imaginable color, creed and non-Aryan origin, fogging up the bag like the windows of a Polish bathhouse.

It's only a shower. Absolute power . . .

I push Luther away and stumble naked through the ruins, back towards blander, less complicated confections, leaving in my wake a trail of rainbow carnage.

Next day, Hansel follows the trail back . . . and lying on my slab are three Milky Ways, a roll of Necco Wafers, some Pop Rocks, and a Giant-Size Sugar Daddy named Luther.

> (HEDWIG *strikes a triumphant pose to a few bars of* Deutschland Über Alles *which segue into . . .)*

SUGAR DADDY

I'VE GOT A SWEET TOOTH
FOR LICORICE DROPS AND JELLY ROLL.
HEY, SUGAR DADDY,
HANSEL NEEDS SOME SUGAR IN HIS BOWL.
I'LL LAY OUT FINE CHINA ON THE LINEN
AND POLISH UP THE CHROME
AND IF YOU GOT SOME SUGAR FOR ME,
SUGAR DADDY, BRING IT HOME.

BLACKSTRAP MOLASSES,
YOU'RE MY ORANGE BLOSSOM HONEY BEAR.
(SUGAR DADDY SUGAR DADDY)
BRING ME VERSACE BLUE JEANS
AND BLACK DESIGNER UNDERWEAR
(SUGAR DADDY SUGAR DADDY)
LET'S DRESS UP LIKE THE DISCO-DANCING JET SET
IN MILAN AND ROME
AND IF YOU GOT SOME SUGAR FOR ME,
SUGAR DADDY, BRING IT HOME.

OH THE THRILL OF CONTROL,
LIKE THE RUSH OF ROCK AND ROLL,
IS THE SWEETEST TASTE I'VE KNOWN,
SO COME ON, SUGAR DADDY, BRING IT HOME.

WHEN HONEY BEES GO SHOPPING
IT'S SOMETHING TO BE SEEN.
(SUGAR DADDY. LICK IT DADDY.)
THEY SWARM TO WILD FLOWERS
AND GET NECTAR FOR THE QUEEN.
(SUGAR DADDY. LICK IT DADDY.)

AND EVERY GIFT YOU BRING ME
GETS ME DRIPPING LIKE A HONEYCOMB
AND IF YOU'VE GOT SOME SUGAR FOR ME,
SUGAR DADDY, BRING IT HOME.

OH THE THRILL OF CONTROL,
LIKE A BLITZKRIEG ON THE ROLL,
IS THE SWEETEST TASTE I'VE KNOWN
SO IF YOU GOT SOME SUGAR,
BRING IT HOME
OH COME ON, SUGAR DADDY, BRING IT HOME!

WHISKEY AND FRENCH CIGARETTES,
A MOTORBIKE WITH HIGH-SPEED JETS
A WATERPIK, A CUISINART
AND A HYPO-ALLERGENIC DOG,
I WANT ALL THE LUXURIES OF THE MODERN AGE,
AND EVERY ITEM ON EVERY PAGE
IN THE LILLIAN VERNON CATALOGUE.

KRZYZHTOFF/YITZHAK (AS LUTHER:)

OH BABY, SOMETHING'S CROSSED MY MIND
AND I WAS THINKING YOU'D LOOK SO FINE
IN A VELVET DRESS
WITH HEELS AND AN ERMINE STOLE.

HEDWIG

OH, LUTHER, DARLING, HEAVEN KNOWS
I'VE NEVER PUT ON WOMEN'S CLOTHES.
EXCEPT FOR ONCE
MY MOTHER'S CAMISOLE.

SO YOU THINK ONLY A WOMAN
CAN TRULY LOVE A MAN
THEN YOU BUY ME THE DRESS,
I'LL BE MORE WOMAN
THAN A MAN LIKE YOU CAN STAND.
I'LL BE YOUR VENUS ON A CHOCOLATE CLAM SHELL
RISING ON A SEA OF MARSHMALLOW FOAM
AND IF YOU GOT SOME SUGAR FOR ME,
SUGAR DADDY, BRING IT HOME.

IT'S OUR TRADITION TO CONTROL,
LIKE ERICH HONECKER AND HELMUT KOHL.
FROM THE UKRAINE TO THE RHONE
SWEET HOME ÜBER ALLES
LORD, I'M COMING HOME.
SO COME ON, SUGAR DADDY, BRING ME HOME.

(Big finish.)

Thank you!

(Looks up hopefully at the man in the box.)
Anything? Any sign of the Bishop, sir? No? Well, if you feel something, say something . . .

(Slips on some sheet music.)

What the hell?

(She picks up a page and reads.)

"Love Theme from The Hurt Locker." *(reading lyrics)* "When the towers fell—" Oh boy. Yitzhak, you speak sight-reading. Do something with this . . .

(YITZHAK takes the music.)

YITZHAK
Can I have a B flat?

HEDWIG
Oh don't worry, you'll be flat.

(YITZHAK starts to sing a terrible Broadway ballad.)

YITZHAK
WE'VE FOUND SANCTUARY IN THE HURT LOCKER
A SPOT OF SAFETY ON THE ROADS
LOVE CAN BE SCARY IN THE HURT . . .
(Turns the page.)
. . . LOCKER

IT'S TENDER AND IT'S RAW
WE'RE FILLED WITH SHOCK AND AWE
AND WE WILL BE CONSUMED WHEN LOVE EXPLODES . . .

HEDWIG

I'm sure it's better in Farsi.

(YITZHAK goes for the money notes.)

YITZHAK

WE WILL BE CONSUMED WHEN LOVE EXPL—

HEDWIG

That'll be enough of that . . .

(YITZHAK is bitter.)

Now what was *I* saying? Yes, Luther and I got married. But it wasn't a traditional wedding. For example, when Luther popped the question, I was on my knees.

(She pulls out a cigarette and heads for the emergency exit door.)

I'm just going to have a quick cig while we talk, is that all right?

I was suddenly the happiest boy in the world. The man I loved would take me away to the land I had only dreamed of. The land of the free, the home of the . . .

(She opens the emergency door for air. The concert barges in.)

44

TOMMY *(Shouting off.)*

—ME. THE REAL ME—

(She slams the door, slowly chews the cigarette and swallows it.)

HEDWIG

I invited Luther home for dinner. After dessert, he produces a ring, an application for American citizenship, and a wig.

(As HANSEL:) "He loves me, Mother. He wants to marry me and get me the hell out of here."

I put the wig on my head. It's a hideous beige shag. "Mother, is this plan so crazy that it just might work?"

Mother's face might have been a photograph it was so still. After what seemed like a lifetime—probably hers—she reaches out her hand to straighten the wig.

(As MOM:) "Get me my passport and my camera, Hansel. I know a certain party."

Yes, the party she'd be having after I left.

(As MOM:) "It's a simple cut and paste job. We change the photo and you can use my name, Hedwig Schmidt."

(AS LUTHER:) "Not so simple, ladies. Baby, you know I love you. I'm always thinking of you. But I got to marry you here. In East Berlin. And that means a full physical examination."

(AS HANSEL:) "Why, they'll see right away that—"

(AS LUTHER:) "Baby. To walk away, you gotta leave something behind. Am I right, Mrs. Schmidt?"

(AS MOM:) "I've always thought so, Luther. Hansel, to be free, one must give up a little part of oneself. And I know just the doctor to take it. Don't move!"

HEDWIG AND THE ANGRY INCH

THE ANGRY INCH

HEDWIG

MY SEX CHANGE OPERATION GOT BOTCHED
MY GUARDIAN ANGEL FELL ASLEEP ON THE WATCH
NOW ALL I GOT IS A BARBIE DOLL CROTCH
I GOT AN ANGRY INCH.

SIX INCHES FORWARD AND FIVE INCHES BACK
I GOT A
I GOT AN ANGRY INCH
SIX INCHES FORWARD AND FIVE INCHES BACK
I GOT A
I GOT AN ANGRY INCH

I'M FROM THE LAND WHERE YOU STILL HEAR THE CRIES
I HAD TO GET OUT, HAD TO SEVER ALL TIES
I CHANGED MY NAME AND ASSUMED A DISGUISE
I GOT AN ANGRY INCH

SIX INCHES FORWARD AND FIVE INCHES BACK
I GOT A
I GOT AN ANGRY INCH
SIX INCHES FORWARD AND FIVE INCHES BACK
I GOT A
I GOT AN ANGRY INCH

47

HEDWIG AND THE ANGRY INCH

SIX INCHES FORWARD AND FIVE INCHES BACK
THE TRAIN IS COMING AND I'M TIED TO THE TRACK
I TRY TO GET UP BUT I CAN'T GET NO SLACK
I GOT A
ANGRY INCH ANGRY INCH

MY MOTHER MADE MY TITS OUT OF CLAY
MY BOYFRIEND TOLD ME THAT HE'D TAKE ME AWAY
THEY DRAGGED ME TO THE DOCTOR ONE DAY
I'VE GOT AN ANGRY INCH

SIX INCHES FORWARD AND FIVE INCHES BACK
I GOT A
I GOT AN ANGRY INCH
SIX INCHES FORWARD AND FIVE INCHES BACK
I GOT A
I GOT AN ANGRY INCH

LONG STORY SHORT
WHEN I WOKE UP FROM THE OPERATION
I WAS BLEEDING DOWN THERE
I WAS BLEEDING FROM THE GASH BETWEEN MY LEGS
MY FIRST DAY AS A WOMAN
AND ALREADY IT'S THAT TIME OF THE MONTH
BUT TWO DAYS LATER
THE HOLE CLOSED UP
THE WOUND HEALED

AND I WAS LEFT WITH A ONE INCH MOUND OF FLESH
WHERE MY PENIS USED TO BE
WHERE MY VAGINA NEVER WAS
A ONE INCH MOUND OF FLESH WITH A SCAR RUNNING
  DOWN IT
LIKE A SIDEWAYS GRIMACE
ON AN EYELESS FACE
JUST A LITTLE BULGE
IT WAS AN ANGRY INCH

SIX INCHES FORWARD AND FIVE INCHES BACK
I GOT A
I GOT AN ANGRY INCH
SIX INCHES FORWARD AND FIVE INCHES BACK
I GOT A
I GOT AN ANGRY INCH

SIX INCHES FORWARD AND FIVE INCHES BACK
THE TRAIN IS COMING AND I'M TIED TO THE TRACK
I TRY TO GET UP BUT I CAN'T GET NO SLACK
I GOT AN
ANGRY INCH ANGRY INCH

SIX INCHES FORWARD AND FIVE INCHES BACK
STAY UNDERCOVER TIL THE NIGHT TURNS TO BLACK
I GOT AN INCH AND I'M SET TO ATTACK
I GOT AN
ANGRY INCH ANGRY INCH

YITZHAK

November 9, 1988. A tiny registrar's office with a breath-taking view over the Wall. Herr Hansel Schmidt becomes Mrs. Hedwig Robinson.

HEDWIG

Tomorrow I am leaving on a jet plane and by the time I get to Phoenix, love will keep us together . . .

(Singing from Helen Reddy's "I Am Woman.")

> ***'CAUSE I'M JUST AN EMBRYO,***
> ***WITH A LONG, LONG WAY TO GO,***
> ***BUT I KNOW TOO MUCH TO GO BACK AND PRETEND!***

YITZHAK

November 9, 1989. Junction City, Kansas.

HEDWIG

I sit in my mobile home, and on bootleg cable, watch the Wall come down . . . divorced, penniless, a woman. I cry, because I will laugh if I don't. Suddenly, I miss Mother. I consider calling Berlin, but then remember with envy her recent escape to sunny Yugoslavia. Perhaps Luther will pick up. No, it's only been a month since he ran off with that bag boy he met on Christianmingle.com. Or whatever we called it back then. Church.

What am I doing? He was never the one. Never the missing half. I catch myself in a mirror and for the first time see clearly the horror hunkering on my head. The same carpet remnant that Luther presented me a year ago to disguise my receding . . . receding . . . I'm receding . . .

I tear the wig from my scalp and hurl it across the room at a pile of unopened anniversary presents.

(Piano intro . . .)

There it lies, feigning shock. My personal hair system. My personal hell. My Hed . . . wig.

WIG IN A BOX

HEDWIG

ON NIGHTS LIKE THIS

WHEN THE WORLD'S A BIT AMISS

AND THE LIGHTS GO DOWN

ACROSS THE TRAILER PARK

I GET DOWN

I FEEL HAD

I FEEL ON THE VERGE OF GOING MAD

AND THEN IT'S TIME TO PUNCH THE CLOCK

I PUT ON SOME MAKE-UP

AND TURN UP THE TAPE DECK

AND PUT THE WIG BACK ON MY HEAD

SUDDENLY I'M MISS MIDWEST

MIDNIGHT CHECKOUT QUEEN

UNTIL I HEAD HOME

AND PUT MYSELF TO BED

I LOOK BACK ON WHERE I'M FROM

LOOK AT THE WOMAN I'VE BECOME

AND THE STRANGEST THINGS

SEEM SUDDENLY ROUTINE

I LOOK UP FROM MY VERMOUTH ON THE ROCKS

A GIFT-WRAPPED WIG STILL IN THE BOX
OF TOWERING VELVETEEN

I PUT ON SOME MAKE-UP
AND SOME LAVERN BAKER
AND PULL THE WIG DOWN FROM THE SHELF
SUDDENLY I'M MISS BEEHIVE 1963
UNTIL I WAKE UP
AND TURN BACK TO MYSELF

SOME GIRLS THEY'VE GOT NATURAL EASE
THEY WEAR IT ANY WAY THEY PLEASE
WITH THEIR FRENCH FLIP CURLS
AND PERFUMED MAGAZINES
WEAR IT UP
LET IT DOWN
THIS IS THE BEST WAY THAT I'VE FOUND
TO BE THE BEST YOU'VE EVER SEEN

I PUT ON SOME MAKE-UP
TURN UP THE EIGHT-TRACK
I'M PULLING THE WIG DOWN FROM THE SHELF
SUDDENLY I'M MISS FARRAH FAWCETT
FROM TV
UNTIL I WAKE UP
AND I TURN BACK TO MYSELF

SHAG, BI-LEVEL, BOB,
DOROTHY HAMILL DO,
SAUSAGE CURLS, CHICKEN WINGS
IT'S ALL BECAUSE OF YOU
WITH YOUR BLOWDRIED, FEATHER BACK,
TONI HOME WAVE, TOO,
FLIP, FRO, FRIZZ, FLOP
IT'S ALL BECAUSE OF YOU
IT'S ALL BECAUSE OF YOU
IT'S ALL BECAUSE OF YOU

(She climbs into the car engine til only her head is visible.)

What do you think, do I give good disembodied head? Ladies and gentlemen, we've reached the most exciting part of the show. The sing-a-long. Totally interactive. Here's what I want you to do. Put down your $75.00 gin and tonic, look up and follow the bouncing balls. Don't worry, they're shaved. Okay . . .

(The lyrics of the chorus are projected for all to sing.)

I PUT ON SOME MAKE-UP
TURN UP THE EIGHT-TRACK
I'M PULLING THE WIG DOWN FROM THE SHELF

*(*HEDWIG *leaps out of the car in a fabulous new dress and wig.)*

SUDDENLY I'M THIS PUNK ROCK STAR

OF STAGE AND SCREEN

AND I AIN'T NEVER

I'M NEVER TURNING BACK

Thank you. I think we have our single!

(Looks up at the man in the box.)

Anything, sir? Were you touched? You felt nothing? Sir, when were you last touched by anybody?

(Turns away.)

Who needs a dead man's approval? We're on a roll!

(Spits liquid into audience.)

That was a rock and roll gesture. Actually that was a heavy metal gesture. Want to see a punk rock gesture?

(Fills mouth; a threatening pause; then she opens her mouth and wets herself.)

HEDWIG

It's the direction of the aggression that defines it. How 'bout this band? On bass, Jacek; on drums, Schlatko; on guitar, Krzyzhtoff, and my trusted musical director, Skszp! Can I buy you a vowel? All so very talented. And so very lucky to be in this country. Right, boys?

BAND *(Sullen.)*

Yes, Miss Hedwig.

HEDWIG

Very good, boys.

*(*YITZHAK *helps her on with a fur coat.)*

Ah, just what I need for perhaps the sweatiest moment in the show.

You like the pelt? Some bitch stopped me on the way in, *(American accent)* "What poor, unfortunate creature had to die for you to wear that?"

"My Aunt Trudi," I replied.

(She turns to YITZHAK. *A large splotch of red paint is revealed on the back of the coat.)*

Have I introduced my husband, Yitzhak? We met during my last Croatian Tour. He was the most famous drag queen in Zagreb. Phyllis thought he would make a great opening act. Billed as "The Last Jewess in the Balkans," he lip-synched something from *Yentl* under the name Krystal Nacht. He was good. He was too good. His applause drowned out my introduction and I refused to go on. But on my way out, he begged me to take him with me. My face might have been my mother's, it was so still. I said to him, "Krystal, to walk away, you gotta leave something behind. I'll marry you on the condition that a wig never touch your head again." He agreed and we've been inseparable ever since. And we'll continue to be. Right, Yitzhak?

(Pointing into the house.)

Look, Yitzhak, Immigration!

*(*YITZHAK *doesn't look.)*

Barbra Streisand!

*(*YITZHAK *can't help but peek.)*

You're no fun, go back to your hole.

*(*YITZHAK *goes.)*

Ladies and Gentlemen, I hope you're becoming fans of Hedwig. Because I find that I am growing deeply accustomed to y—

*(*YITZHAK *kicks open the emergency door.)*

TOMMY *(Off.)*

. . . one day, this little trailer trash kid put on some of his mom's eyeliner, grabbed his beat-up J.C. Penney guitar and called himself Tommy Gnosis!

(HEDWIG howls into the cheering crowd.)

HEDWIG

TOMMY, CAN YOU HEAR ME? FROM THIS MILKLESS TIT, YOU SUCKED THE VERY BUSINESS WE CALL SHOW!

(Slams the door.)

Okay. Okay. You want to know about Tommy Gnosis? I'll tell you about Tommy Gnosis. Get this dead thing off of me.

(YITZHAK removes her coat. HEDWIG turns to the band and snaps . . .)

Leute, wir improvisieren jetzt! Bleib dran!

After my divorce, I scraped by for many years with babysitting gigs and odd jobs. Mostly the jobs we call blow. I had lost my job at the base PX and I had lost my gag reflex. You do the math. I sat for the baby of General Speck, commander of the nearby Army fort. His other son was The Artist Formerly Known As My Buttboy.

Yes, Tommy Speck. Tommy was a seventeen-year-old, four-eyed, pock-marked, Dungeon and Dragons-obsessed Jesus freak with a fish on his truck and I found him incredibly . . . hot.

Perhaps it was his disdain for authority, his struggle with organized religion. One day, I walked in on him, punishing the bishop. He was in the bath with the door wide open, clearly waiting for me. I reached down, finished His Grace off, and dropped a flyer in the water. "By the way, Tommy, I am performing a short set tonight at Dr. Espresso's Seattle-Style Coffee Enema Bar. Maybe I'll see you there."

I had recently returned to my first love, music. I had tried singing once back in Berlin. They threw tomatoes. After the show I had a nice salad. But newly motivated, I bought a cheap electric piano . . .

(Cheesy piano phrase.)

HEDWIG

And I found a couple of Korean sargeants' wives who churned out a mean rhythm section . . .

(Bad drums.)

We became quite a draw singing the hits of the day under the name The Angry Inch.

(Guitar sting. Projection of Dr. Espresso's logo.)

That night the audience was small, but hostile.

(Lounge version of a late-era grunge song winds down. She speaks to Dr. Espresso's audience.)

Thank you. Both of you. That was another one by Creed. How 'bout Kwang-Yi on guitar? Give it up! Kwang-Yi!

(Bad guitar solo.)

Give it up, Kwang.

(She sees someone in the audience.)

Looks like we have a celebrity here tonight over by the Sweet & Low. Ladies and gentlemen, little Tommy Speck, the General's son!

(Band claps half-heartedly. To TOMMY re: the applause.)

That's more than I got, honey. He's embarrassed.

(Piano intro starts.)

Well, I'm a little nervous myself. This is the first song I've ever written. And it's written for a guy to sing. We're talking to John Mayer's people. But then again, aren't we all?

WICKED LITTLE TOWN

HEDWIG

YOU KNOW, THE SUN IS IN YOUR EYES
AND HURRICANES AND RAINS
AND BLACK AND CLOUDY SKIES.

YOU'RE RUNNING UP AND DOWN THAT HILL.
YOU TURN IT ON AND OFF AT WILL.
THERE'S NOTHING HERE TO THRILL
OR BRING YOU DOWN.
AND IF YOU'VE GOT NO OTHER CHOICE
YOU KNOW YOU CAN FOLLOW MY VOICE
THROUGH THE DARK TURNS AND NOISE
OF THIS WICKED LITTLE TOWN.

OH LADY, LUCK HAS LED YOU HERE
AND THEY'RE SO TWISTED UP
THEY'LL TWIST YOU UP. I FEAR

THE PIOUS, HATEFUL AND DEVOUT,
YOU'RE TURNING TRICKS TIL YOU'RE TURNED OUT,
THE WIND SO COLD IT BURNS,
YOU'RE BURNING OUT AND BLOWING ROUND
AND IF YOU'VE GOT NO OTHER CHOICE
YOU KNOW YOU CAN FOLLOW MY VOICE

THROUGH THE DARK TURNS AND NOISE
OF THIS WICKED LITTLE TOWN.

THE FATES ARE VICIOUS AND THEY'RE CRUEL.
YOU LEARN TOO LATE YOU'VE USED TWO WISHES
LIKE A FOOL

AND THEN YOU'RE SOMEONE YOU ARE NOT,
AND JUNCTION CITY AIN'T THE SPOT.
REMEMBER MRS. LOT
AND WHEN SHE TURNED AROUND.
AND IF YOU GOT NO OTHER CHOICE
YOU KNOW YOU CAN FOLLOW MY VOICE
THROUGH THE DARK TURNS AND NOISE
OF THIS WICKED LITTLE TOWN.

(On the final chord, she blows a kiss to TOMMY. *She dabs her face with a towel and looks down at it. She holds it up.)*

HEDWIG AND THE ANGRY INCH

HEDWIG

Ladies and Gentlemen, the shroud of Hedwig.

(She throws it into the audience.)

The next day, I was putting the little Speck baby to bed when Tommy appeared with a expensive-looking electric guitar.

(As TOMMY:) "Your show . . . that song . . . my dad . . . gave me this guitar to apologize for being a pathetic little dictator . . . You want to come up to my room?"

We went up to the attic and he sang me songs. "Classics," I was informed. The bands were new to me: Boston, Kansas, America, Europe, Asia. I put my hand on his strings.

(As HEDWIG:) "Travel exhausts me."

(As TOMMY:) "Where are you from, Hedwig?"

I told him my story. His face might have been a Yes album cover it was so still.

(As TOMMY:) "Have you accepted Jesus Christ, the Son of God, as your Lord and personal savior?"

(As HEDWIG:) "No, but I love His work."

(As TOMMY:) "You know, what He saved us from was His fucking father. I mean what kind of God creates Adam in His image, pulls Eve out of him to keep him company, and then tells them not to eat from the Tree of Knowledge? That was so micromanaging. So was Adam. But Eve. Eve just wanted to know shit. She took a bite of the apple and found out what was good and what was evil. And she gave it to Adam so he would know. Because they were in love. And that was good, they now knew. Hedwig, will you give me the apple?"

The words spilling from those lips. And his eyes. His irises were clear cylinders of surprising depth. And emptiness. Only a few puddles of bluish pain sloshed around inside. Same blue as my eyes.

At the time, Tommy's performance options were limited to the occasional guitar mass. I initiated a six-month curriculum of rock history, lyrics, grooming and vocal training—my patented . . . *(Reverb.)* . . . oven technique.

For his graduation, I gave him his name, Tommy Gnosis . . .

("Gnosis" logo is projected.)

. . . the Greek word for knowledge. We collaborated. Songs exploded out of us. He started singing backup for me at Dr. Espresso's. Teenage girls started showing up.

(YITZHAK *emits a hysterical girl giggle.*)

I added a few duets. Standing-room only. Then, The Sizzler called. Had The Sizzler ever called anyone before? Next thing we knew, we were in the middle of a year-long residency next to the salad bar. In a matter of months, we were outgrossing monster trucks in Wichita. With that kind of money pouring in, I was able to give up all my jobs and devote myself entirely to our career. We were very happy.

One day, I am curled up in the trailer with my usual late afternoon constitutional of grain alcohol and Brita. I like to be good to myself. Suddenly, Tommy is at the door in tears.

(AS HEDWIG:) "Honey, what is it?"

(AS TOMMY:) "My dad . . . and my mom . . . and my parents."

I hold him. As I never had been held. But as usual he squirms, slides behind me and clutches my spine to his chest. I am suddenly very much aware that we haven't kissed in all the months we've been together. In fact, he has maintained a near-perfect ignorance of the front of me.

(As HEDWIG:) "Honey, why don't you work on that new song while I finish shaving your eyebrows?"

(TOMMY *strums a guitar chord.*)

(TOMMY *sings:*) *"LOOK WHAT YOU DONE . . ."*

(*Bad chord.*)

(As TOMMY*:)* "Shit."

Another song blows in from the trailer next door.

YITZHAK

(*Gently sings chorus to "I Will Always Love You" à la Whitney Houston.*)

. . . AND IIIIIIII . . .

HEDWIG

This song has been playing on a loop for three days.

YITZHAK

. . . WILL ALWAYS LOVE YOU.
I WILL ALWAYS LOVE YOU . . .

(YITZHAK *continues through the following.*)

HEDWIG

Tommy looks up at me through new lenses, one blue and one pink.

(AS TOMMY:) "What do you think? Does love last forever?"

(AS HEDWIG:) "No, but this song does."

(AS TOMMY:) "Do not knock a multi-platinum single. I wish I could hit those notes."

(AS HEDWIG:) "Just move your lips and I'll sing them for you, honey. From a shadowy corner of the stage. Like Mick Jagger's backup singer."

We laugh at the professional reference and I return to his brows.

(AS HEDWIG:) "Seriously, Tom, yes. I believe love is immortal."

(TOMMY *strums the same guitar chord again.*)

(TOMMY *sings:)* "*LOOK WHAT YOU DONE . . .*"

(*Another bad chord change.*)

(As TOMMY:) "Goddammit! How is it immortal?"

(As HEDWIG:) "Well, perhaps because love creates something that was not there before."

(As TOMMY:) "What, like procreation?"

(As HEDWIG:) "Yes, but not only."

(As TOMMY:) "What, like recreation?"

He grabs my ass and he laughs. I don't.

(As HEDWIG:) "Sometimes just creation. Don't move."

I paint a bold silver cross on his forehead.

(TOMMY strums the chord.)

(As HEDWIG:) "Honey, have you thought of a D after that E flat?"

(TOMMY SINGS:) ***LOOK WHAT YOU DONE—**"*

(The D works.)

YITZHAK *(The big chorus.)*

AND IIIIIIII . . . !

Tommy slowly rises and draws the curtains that are attached at the top and the bottom. He reaches out his hand. I take it and I am filled with an ancient clarity.

(The "Origin of Love" chords drift in.)

He's the one . . .

(Projection of the broken eye.)

No blood in my eyes, no blood on his face. He's the one. The one who was taken. The one who left. The twin born by fission. He'll die in fusion. Our fusion, cold fusion, unlimited power, unlimited knowledge. The secrets he must hold, the memories that we shared. The words to complete the sentence that I began, "I am—!" My eyes fill with muddy Maybelline tears.

(As TOMMY:) "Oh, Hedwig. Oh, God. When Eve was still inside Adam, they were in Paradise. When she was pulled from him, that's when Paradise was lost. So when she enters him again, Paradise will be regained!"

(As HEDWIG:) "However you want it, honey, just kiss me while we do it."

I wrench his body around to face mine and thrust his hand between my le—

(As TOMMY:) "What is that?"

(Pause)

(As HEDWIG:) "That's what I have to work with."

(Pause)

(As TOMMY:) "My mom is probably wondering where I—"

(As HEDWIG:) "You fucking sissy. What are you afraid of?"

(As TOMMY:) "I love you."

(As HEDWIG:) "*Then love the front of me.*"

He runs out the back door.

(The guitar intro to "The Long Grift" begins. HEDWIG *tries to sing but cannot. She walks away from the spotlight. Confusion among the band.* YITZHAK *walks up to the mic and begins to sing the song.)*

THE LONG GRIFT

YITZHAK

LOOK WHAT YOU'VE DONE,
YOU GIGOLO.
YOU KNOW THAT I LOVED YOU, HON,
AND I DIDN'T WANT TO KNOW
THAT YOUR COOL,
SEDUCTIVE SERENADE
WAS A TOOL
OF YOUR TRADE,
YOU GIGOLO.

OF ALL THE RICHES YOU'VE SURVEYED,
AND ALL THAT YOU CAN LIFT,
I'M JUST ANOTHER DOLLAR THAT YOU MADE
IN YOUR LONG, LONG GRIFT

(HEDWIG *begins singing backup.*)

YITZHAK

LOOK WHAT YOU'VE DONE,
YOU GIGOLO.
ANOTHER HUSTLE HAS BEEN RUN,
AND NOW YOU OUGHT TO KNOW

THAT THIS FOOL
CAN NO LONGER BE SWAYED
BY THE TOOLS
OF YOUR TRADE,
YOU GIGOLO.

I'M JUST ANOTHER JOHN YOU'VE GYPPED,
ANOTHER SUCKER STIFFED,
A WALK ON ROLE IN THE SCRIPT
TO YOUR LONG, LONG GRIFT.
THE LOVE THAT HAD ME IN YOUR GRIP
WAS JUST A LONG, LONG GRIFT.

HEDWIG

It's nice over here. Out of the spotlight. Singing gentle backup harmonies in my oven. *(To* YITZHAK.*)* You were good. They seemed to like you. Maybe there's enough room for both of us in this act.

(She touches YITZHAK *who stands motionless.)*

The German and the Jew. Think of the symmetry. Think of the publicity. Think of the pow—

*(*YITZHAK *spits in her face and walks away.*

HEDWIG *is alone.)*

HEDWIG'S LAMENT

HEDWIG

I WAS BORN ON THE OTHER SIDE
OF A TOWN RIPPED IN TWO
AND NO MATTER HOW HARD I'VE TRIED
I END UP BLACK AND BLUE

I ROSE FROM OFF OF THE DOCTOR'S SLAB
I LOST A PIECE OF MY HEART
NOW EVERYONE GETS TO TAKE A STAB
THEY CUT ME UP INTO PARTS

I GAVE A PIECE TO MY MOTHER
I GAVE A PIECE TO MY MAN
I GAVE A PIECE TO THE ROCK STAR
HE TOOK THE GOOD STUFF AND RAN

EXQUISITE CORPSE

HEDWIG

OH GOD
I'M ALL SEWN UP
A HARDENED RAZOR CUT
SCAR MAP ACROSS MY BODY
AND YOU CAN TRACE THE LINES
THROUGH MISERY'S DESIGNS
THAT MAP ACROSS MY BODY

HEDWIG, YITZHAK, BAND

A COLLAGE
ALL SEWN UP
A MONTAGE
ALL SEWN UP

JACEK AND YITZHAK

A RANDOM PATTERN WITH A NEEDLE AND THREAD
THE OVERLAPPING WAY DISEASES ARE SPREAD
THROUGH A TORNADO BODY
WITH A HAND GRENADE HEAD
AND THE LEGS ARE TWO LOVERS ENTWINED

HEDWIG

INSIDE I'M HOLLOWED OUT
OUTSIDE'S A PAPER SHROUD
AND ALL THE REST'S ILLUSION

THAT THERE'S A WILL AND SOUL
THAT WE CAN WREST CONTROL
FROM CHAOS AND CONFUSION

HEDWIG, YITZHAK, BAND

A COLLAGE
ALL SEWN UP
A MONTAGE
ALL SEWN UP

HEDWIG, YITZHAK, SKSZP, KRZYZHTOFF

THE AUTOMATIST'S UNDOING
THE WHOLE WORLD STARTS UNSCREWING
AS TIME COLLAPSES AND SPACE WARPS
YOU SEE DECAY AND RUIN
I TELL YOU "NO, NO, NO, NO
YOU MAKE SUCH AN EXQUISITE CORPSE"

HEDWIG

I'VE GOT IT ALL SEWN UP
A HARDENED RAZOR CUT
SCAR MAP ACROSS MY BODY
AND YOU CAN TRACE THE LINES
THROUGH MISERY'S DESIGNS
THAT MAP ACROSS MY BODY

HEDWIG, YITZHAK, BAND

A COLLAGE
ALL SEWN UP
A MONTAGE
ALL SEWN UP . . .

(Strobes. She tears off her wig, rips open her dress and pulls two tomatoes from her bra. She smashes them on her chest, grabs a bottle of alcohol from YITZHAK, *swigs it, pours the rest over her head.* YITZHAK *wrestles for the bottle. A melee.* HEDWIG *disappears as* YITZHAK *shoves the band away to grab the discarded wig and then throw it to the ground. He falls to his knees and crumples in despair. The music crescendos, disintegrates and crossfades to stadium-sized cheers. The piano intro to "Wicked Little Town" begins.)*

TOMMY *(Off.)*

Before I go, I'd like to sing a song that someone wrote for me a long time ago. I don't know where she is tonight. But if you're real quiet . . . maybe she can hear me.

*(*HEDWIG *rises into new light. Her wig is gone and a bold silver cross shines across her forehead. She has become* TOMMY *in concert.)*

WICKED LITTLE TOWN (REPRISE)

HEDWIG *(As TOMMY)*

FORGIVE ME,
FOR I DID NOT KNOW
'CAUSE I WAS JUST A BOY
AND YOU WERE SO MUCH MORE

THAN ANY GOD COULD EVER PLAN,
MORE THAN A WOMAN OR A MAN.
AND NOW I UNDERSTAND
HOW MUCH I TOOK FROM YOU:
THAT, WHEN EVERYTHING STARTS BREAKING DOWN,
YOU TAKE THE PIECES OFF THE GROUND
AND SHOW THIS WICKED TOWN
SOMETHING BEAUTIFUL AND NEW.

YOU THINK THAT LUCK
HAS LEFT YOU THERE.
BUT MAYBE THERE'S NOTHING
UP IN THE SKY BUT AIR.

AND THERE'S NO MYSTICAL DESIGN,
NO COSMIC LOVER PREASSIGNED.
THERE'S NOTHING YOU CAN FIND
THAT CANNOT BE FOUND.

'CAUSE WITH ALL THE CHANGES
YOU'VE BEEN THROUGH,
IT SEEMS THE STRANGER'S ALWAYS YOU,
ALONE AGAIN IN SOME NEW
WICKED LITTLE TOWN.

SO, WHEN YOU'VE GOT NO OTHER CHOICE
YOU KNOW YOU CAN FOLLOW MY VOICE
THROUGH THE DARK TURNS AND NOISE
OF THIS WICKED LITTLE TOWN.
OH, IT'S A WICKED LITTLE TOWN.
GOODBYE, WICKED LITTLE TOWN.

(The song ends and stark bright light fills the stage. Silence. She is not sure where she is. Or even who she is. She see her wig on the floor and picks it up. She wipes her forehead and finds silver makeup on her hand. Pause. Finally, she looks to the guitarist who begins to play.)

MIDNIGHT RADIO

HEDWIG

RAIN FALLS HARD
BURNS DRY
A DREAM
OR A SONG
THAT HITS YOU SO HARD
FILLING YOU UP
AND SUDDENLY GONE

(She holds the wig out to YITZHAK. *He takes it with resignation and begins to put it on* HEDWIG*'s head.* HEDWIG *stops him and gently pushes the wig back.* YITZHAK *hesitates, then understanding, places the wig on his own head.)*

BREATHE FEEL LOVE
GIVE FREE
KNOW IN YOUR SOUL
LIKE YOUR BLOOD KNOWS THE WAY
FROM YOUR HEART TO YOUR BRAIN
KNOW THAT YOU'RE WHOLE

(HEDWIG *takes* YITZHAK*'s hand. They sway together. She releases his hand, setting him free.* YITZHAK *slowly descends the stage and exits into the house with the grace of new hope.)*

AND YOU'RE SHINING
LIKE THE BRIGHTEST STAR
A TRANSMISSION
ON THE MIDNIGHT RADIO
AND YOU'RE SPINNING
LIKE A 45
BALLERINA
DANCING TO YOUR ROCK AND ROLL,

HERE'S TO PATTI
    AND TINA
    AND YOKO
       ARETHA
    AND NONA
    AND NICO
    AND ME.

AND ALL THE STRANGE ROCK-AND-ROLLERS
YOU KNOW YOU'RE DOING ALL RIGHT
SO HOLD ON TO EACH OTHER
YOU GOTTA HOLD ON TONIGHT

AND YOU'RE SHINING
LIKE THE BRIGHTEST STARS
A TRANSMISSION
ON THE MIDNIGHT RADIO

AND YOU'RE SPINNING
YOUR NEW 45'S
ALL THE MISFITS AND THE LOSERS.
YEAH, YOU KNOW YOU'RE ROCK AND ROLLERS
SPINNING TO YOUR ROCK AND ROLL

LIFT UP YOUR HANDS
LIFT UP YOUR HANDS
LIFT UP YOUR HANDS
LIFT UP YOUR HANDS

(YITZHAK *reappears dressed in stunning female drag and mounts the stage singing.*)

HEDWIG AND YITZHAK

LIFT UP YOUR HANDS
LIFT UP YOUR HANDS
LIFT UP YOUR HANDS
LIFT UP YOUR HANDS . . .

(*An enormous upstage loading door opens. Bright light and cheers.* HEDWIG *walks slowly into the light and disappears.* YITZHAK *and the band continue . . .*)

LIFT UP YOUR HANDS

LIFT UP YOUR HANDS

LIFT UP YOUR HANDS

LIFT UP YOUR HANDS . . .

(The broken eye from "The Origin of Love" appears and, as the song ends . . .

. . . it merges and becomes whole.)

END

SELECTED VERSES from
THE GOSPEL OF THOMAS*

His disciples said to him, "Is circumcision beneficial?" Jesus said to them, "If it were beneficial, their father would beget them from their mother already circumcised. Rather, it is the true circumcision of the spirit that has proved entirely profitable."

Jesus said to them, "When you make the two into one, and the inside like the outside and the outside like the inside, and the above like the below, and when you make the male and the female into one and the same, so that the male be not male nor the female female; and when you fashion eyes in place of an eye, a hand in place of a hand, a foot in place of a foot, and a likeness in place of a likeness; then you will enter the kingdom."

Jesus said, "Do not fret from morning until evening and from evening until morning about what you will wear."

Jesus said, "If you bring forth what is within you, what you bring forth will save you. If you do not bring forth what is within you, what you do not bring forth will destroy you."

*One of the Gnostic gospels from the first century A.D., which were deemed unsuitable for inclusion in the New Testament by the early Christian church.

ARISTOPHANES' SPEECH
from PLATO'S *SYMPOSIUM*

In the first place, let me treat of the nature of man and what
has happened to it; for the original human nature was not
like the present, but different. The sexes were not two as
they are now, but originally three in number; there was man,
woman and the union of the two, having a name corre-
sponding to this double nature, which had once a real exis-
tence, but is now lost, and the word "Androgynous" is only
preserved as a term of reproach. In the second place, the
primeval man was round, his back and sides forming a cir-
cle; and he had four hands and four feet, one head with two
faces, looking opposite ways, set on a round neck and pre-
cisely alike; also four ears, two privy members, and the
remainder to correspond. He could walk upright as men now
do, backwards or forwards as he pleased, and he could also
roll over and over at a great pace, turning on his four hands
and four feet, eight in all, like tumblers going over and over

with their legs in the air; this was when he wanted to run fast. Now the sexes were three; and such as I have described them; because the sun, moon and earth are three and the man was originally the child of the sun, the woman of the earth, and the man-woman of the moon, which is made up of sun and earth, and they were all round and moved round and round like their parents. Terrible was their might and strength, and the thoughts of their hearts were great, and they made an attack upon the gods; of them is told the tale of Otys and Ephialtes who, as Homer says, dared to scale heaven, and would have laid hands upon the gods. Doubt reigned in the celestial councils. Should they kill them and annihilate the race with thunderbolts, as they had done the giants, then there would be an end of the sacrifices and worship which men offered to them; but, on the other hand, the gods could not suffer their insolence to be unrestrained. At last, after a good deal of reflection, Zeus discovered a way. He said: "Methinks I have a plan which will humble their pride and improve their manners; men shall continue to exist, but I will cut them in two and then they will be diminished in strength and increased in numbers; this will have the advantage of making them more profitable to us. They shall walk upright on two legs, and if they continue insolent and will not be quiet, I will split them again, and they shall hop about on a single leg." He spoke and cut men in two, like a sorb-apple which is halved for pickling, or as you might divide an egg with a hair; and as he cut them one after another, he bade Apollo give the face and the half of the neck a turn in order that the man might contemplate the section of himself: he would thus learn a lesson of humility. Apollo was also bidden to heal their wounds and compose their forms. So he gave a turn to the face and pulled the skin from the sides all over that which in our language is called the belly, like the purses which draw in, and he made one mouth at the center, which he fastened in a knot (the same which is called the navel); he also molded the breast and took out most of the wrinkles, much as a shoemaker might smooth leather upon a last; he left a few, however, in the region of the belly and navel, as a memorial of the primeval state. After the division the two parts of man, each desiring his other half, came together, and throwing their arms about one another, entwined in mutual embraces, longing to grow into one, they were on the point of dying from hunger and self-neglect, because they did not like to do anything apart; and when one of the halves died and the other survived, the survivor sought another mate, man or woman as we call them,—being the sections of entire men or women,—and clung to that. They were being destroyed, when Zeus in pity of them invented a new plan: he turned the parts of generation round to the front, for this had not been always their position, and they sowed the seed no longer as hitherto like grasshoppers in the ground, but in one another; and after the transposition the male generated in the female in order that by the mutual embraces of man

and woman they might breed, and the race might continue;
or if man came to man they might be satisfied, and rest, and
go their ways to the business of life: so ancient is the desire
of one another which is implanted in us, reuniting our original nature, making one of two, and healing the state of man.
Each of us when separated, having one side only, like a flat
fish, is but the indenture of a man, and he is always looking
for his other half. Men who are a section of that double
nature which was once called Androgynous are lovers of
women; adulterers are generally of this breed, and also
adulterous women who lust after men: the women who are
a section of the woman do not care for men, but have
female attachments; the female companions are of this sort.
But they who are a section of the male follow the male, and
while they are young, being slices of the original man, they
hang about men and embrace them, and they are them-
selves the best of boys and youths, because they have the
most manly nature. Some indeed assert that they are
shameless, but this is not true: for they do not act thus from
any want of shame, but because they are valiant and manly,
and have a manly countenance, and they embrace that
which is like them. And these when they grow up become
our statesmen, and these only, which is a great proof of the
truth of what I am saying. When they reach manhood they
are lovers of youth, and are not naturally inclined to marry
or beget children,—if at all, they do so only in obedience to
the law; but they are satisfied if they may be allowed to live

with one another unwedded; and such a nature is prone to love and ready to return love, always embracing that which is akin to him. And when one of them meets with his other half, the actual half of himself, whether he be a lover of youth or a lover of another sort, the pair are lost in amazement of love and friendship and intimacy, and one will not be out of the other's sight, as I may say, even for a moment: these are the people who pass their whole lives together; yet they could not explain what they desire of one another. For the intense yearning which each of them has towards the other does not appear to be the desire of lover's intercourse, but of something else which the soul of either evidently desires and cannot tell, and of which she has only a dark and doubtful presentiment. Suppose Hephaestus, with his instruments, to come to the pair who are lying side by side and to say to them, "What do you people want of one another?" they would be unable to explain. And suppose further, that when he saw their perplexity he said: "Do you desire to be wholly one; always day and night to be in one another's company? For if this is what you desire, I am ready to melt you into one and let you grow together, so that being two you shall become one, and while you live a common life as if you were a single man, and after your death in the world below still be one departed soul instead of two—I ask whether this is what you lovingly desire,—and whether you are satisfied to attain this?"—there is not a man of them who when he heard the proposal would deny or would not acknowledge that this meeting and melting into one another, this becoming one instead of two, was the very expression of his ancient need. And the reason is that human nature was originally one and we were a whole, and the desire and pursuit of the whole is called love. There was a time, I say, when we were one, but now because of the wickedness of mankind God has dispersed us, as the Arcadians were dispersed into villages by the Lacedaemonians. And if we are not obedient to the gods, there is a danger that we shall be split up again and go about in bas relief, like the profile figures having only half a nose which are sculptured on monuments, and that we shall be like tallies. Wherefore let us exhort all men to piety, that we may avoid evil, and obtain the good, of which love is to us the lord and minister; and let no one oppose him—he is the enemy of the gods who opposes him. For if we are friends of the God and at peace with him we shall find our own true loves. I believe that if our loves were perfectly accomplished, and each one returning to his primeval nature had his original true love, then our race would be happy.

Translated by Benjamin Jowett